Pages 2 and 3:
Photo by
Bruce Crook

Pages 34 and 35:
Photo by
Isabelle Francais

T.F.H.
Publications,
The Spinney,
Parklands,
Denmead,
Portsmouth
PO7 6AR
England

t.f.h.

Your First
RABBIT

Louise Vernier

Introduction

The March Hare, Peter Cottontail, Thumper, Br'er Rabbit, Bugs Bunny, Peter Rabbit . . . Who at some time in his life hasn't listened with delight to a story about one of the many famous rabbits that have captured the imagination of children and grownups the world over? And how many youngsters haven't searched through the house, hunting for those marvelous eggs and gaily colored baskets of goodies left by that most famous of all rabbits—the Easter Bunny?

The tales and legends of all these famous rabbits were inspired by an extraordinary, yet everyday, little fellow whose great appeal makes him one of the finest pets around.

A rabbit, in fact, may be just the kind of pet you are looking for. Being a rather compact creature, he requires little in the way of space, and he can make a fine indoor, as well as outdoor, pet.

Lunching as he does chiefly on grains and greens, he is amazingly inexpensive to keep. To take care of him is not difficult; he is one of the cleanest animals alive—even a white bunny somehow stays a snowy white with little help from anyone. A rabbit, being gentle by nature, will warm up to you quickly. And don't be surprised if your lap becomes his favorite resting place.

He loves people and people love him. Quick-witted and affectionate, he has become a popular pet in big cities and in small towns. The rabbit does not require as much time and care as do many other kinds of domesticated pets, yet he offers much. The rabbit is indeed a likable little fellow who has created a faithful following throughout the land. And to top-off all his other desirable attributes, he makes no noise to disturb the neighbors.

Rabbits are curious, attentive little animals with an irresistible charm all their own; they are hard to beat when it comes to the ideal small pet.

History

The rabbit, looking much as he does today, existed long before the dawn of recorded history. It was not until about 1000 BC, however, that he actually gets a written notice from the Phoenician traders of the Mediterranean. On their journeys to what is now Spain, these seagoing merchants noticed the abundance of a timid little animal who lived in burrows. They transported some of these unknown animals on their sailing voyages to other parts of Europe, and soon they became a common sight in most of the Mediterranean lands, from where they began to spread out in all directions.

The Romans proved industrious in containing their rabbit herds—stone walls were erected to confine these hoppingly prolific and intriguing animals. The ancients were impressed by the propagation propensity of rabbits and believed that their flesh brought beauty and fertility to their women.

RABBITS AS PETS

It appears that domesticated rabbits were being raised as pets in a few monasteries in France somewhere around the sixth century. It was not until the sixteenth century, however, that rabbits began to catch on as pets. It has been during more recent times, especially the last several decades, that rabbits have really come into their own. Today, without doubt, they can be included among the most popular of pet animals.

National rabbit-registering organizations can be credited with helping to promote the rabbit's role in the pet world. The members of these various organizations, dedicated to the highest standards of rabbit keeping, have worked diligently to foster the development of countless breeds of rabbit. Additionally, they have been notably successful in their efforts to educate and inform rabbit keepers who are new to the hobby.

CLASSIFICATION

Because of their long incisor teeth, rabbits are thought of by many people as belonging to the scientific order that includes mice, hamsters, gerbils, and other rodents. However, rabbits differ from these animals in that they have *two* pairs of incisors, placed one behind the other. This characteristic puts them in the scientific order called Lagomorpha, which also includes pikas and hares.

It is from the species *Oryctolagus cuniculus* that all present-day domestic varieties of rabbit, including their many sizes, shapes, and colors, were developed.

Clean, quiet, and relatively easy to keep, a rabbit can make a fine pet. The more familiar you are with a rabbit's needs and behavior, the more successful you will be as a rabbit keeper. Photo by Michael Gilroy.

Rabbits come in a wide variety of sizes, shapes, and colors—something for everyone! This five-week-old youngster exhibits the charm that has won the hearts of many fanciers. Photo by Michael Gilroy.

Selection

Many of the names given to rabbits are quite exotic—like Dutch and Himalayan—but these names usually have no connection with the rabbit's real home, for all the tame rabbits we have today are descended from those early wild ones of Europe.

There are rabbits as big as spaniels; there are rabbits as small as guinea pigs. In between, there are rabbits of every size, shape, and color—more than fifty domestic breeds from which to choose your pet. If this figure overwhelms you, find out from a pet shop dealer the best breed for you. Buy your pet. You may love that wild rabbit you caught, but a wild rabbit, even a baby one, is difficult to raise. It's best to leave him where you found him.

Although it is not possible to present every rabbit breed that is available, the following breed discussion gives the reader a thorough overview of some of the types of rabbit that are available to the hobbyist.

Dutch: This fellow is colored similarly fore and aft, with a broad band of white "painted" around his middle. Available in a variety of attractive colors and possessing a charming disposition, it is no wonder that this small to medium character with his charming disposition has become so popular a pet.

Polish: Imagine a shimmering white rabbit, not much bigger than a chihuahua, with bright, expressive eyes (blue or ruby colored) and you have the Polish. He is also available in a number of other lovely colors. Some Polish rabbits can be high strung and a bit snappish, but fanciers of the breed maintain that to know one is to love one.

Belgian Hare: One of the most intelligent of rabbits. This attractive animal, whose weight can range from six to ten pounds, has beautiful, lush fur that is reddish tan in color.

Himalayan: This pink-eyed rabbit sports a white coat with markings that are black or blue in color. Ideally, these markings are on the nose, ears, tail, feet, and legs. Medium in size, he weighs from two to four pounds.

Angora: These beautiful rabbits are easily recognizable by the distinctive quality of their coats. The English Angora can be distinguished from the French Angora by the abundant furnishings (fringes and tassels) on his ears. Additionally, the English Angora is somewhat smaller than the French Angora. Both of these breeds are available in white and a variety of other colors. Compared to some other types of rabbit, the Angora is more difficult to take care of, but if you devote the necessary time and patience to brush, clean, and clip him, you will be rewarded by the beauty of this prized and unusual pet.

Lop: The hallmark of lop rabbits is their long, soft, dropping or "lop" ears (which in some lop breeds are enormous in size in relation to body size). In the larger lop breeds, ear-lengths can easily measure over 20 inches. The English Lop and the French Lop come in a variety of solid and broken colors.

If you love the look of a lop rabbit but want a relatively small pet, the Mini Lop may be just what you you're looking for. These rabbits, with all the charm and appeal of their bigger cousins, weigh an average four and one-half to five and one-half pounds. You might also want to consider the pint-sized lop rabbit known as the Holland Lop. These cute little characters average around three pounds in weight.

Silver: These beautiful rabbits are the choice of quite a few hobbyists. Silvers, whose coats are short and even in length, are available in several colors, all of which are highlighted by the breed's characteristic silvering. Adult members of the breed average in weight between four to seven pounds.

Netherland Dwarf: These rabbits, often simply called dwarf rabbits, are a favorite of many in the fancy. Their appearance is quite distinctive: short ears perched atop an apple-round head and a very compact body. Netherland Dwarfs, which come in a beautiful variety of colors, are known for their even dispositions.

Chinchilla: There are three recognized breeds of Chinchillas: the Giant, American and Standard. The distinguishing characteristic of all three breeds is the unique color, "to resemble real chinchilla." The undercolor is a dark slate blue at the base, light pearl at the center, and the top banded in black; the chinchilla effect is accomplished by a very light band brightly ticked with jet black hairs in a wavy fashion. Otherwise these three breeds differ principally in size; their attractive coats and larger size attract both fanciers and farmers.

English Spot: In an attractive array of colors, the English comes to modern-day fanciers from a long line of British-bred bunnies, with earliest references from the mid-nineteenth century. This racy rabbit is streaked with distinct markings, which run deep toward the skin. Among its features include the butterfly, whose wings hover over the whisker beds, and the herringbone spine markings, clearly traceable and unblotched. The English Spot's hallmark, however, is the chain of spots which appear along each side of the flanks. In a faultless specimen, the spots are distinct, untouching, and gracefully sweeping.

Havana: A furry Dutch bunny, once dubbed the beaver, the Havana has been a well-known European breed since the turn of the century, exhibited widely in France, Switzerland, Germany, Holland, and England. Its present name derives

Netherland Dwarf rabbit. Members of this breed are among the smallest of all rabbits, weighing from two to two-and-one-half pounds. Photo by Isabelle Francais.

A black Tan rabbit. Other color varieties of the breed are blue, chocolate, and lilac. Photo by Isabelle Francais.

from the brown variety's close color resemblance to the Cuban cigar. Short and cobby and wholly romantic, the Havana has dark eyes that twinkle a rich ruby glow in a darkened room. The fur is approximately an inch in length and comes in black and blue, in addition to Havana chocolate.

Flemish Giant: This is a long and powerful rabbit whose body is notably square and wide. Color, which is always uniform, can be any solid except white. As its name suggests, this rabbit blossomed in Flanders, Belgium, where it was known as the Patagonian and favored for its tremendous size. The coat on the Flemish is strikingly full and bright, and always of one length.

Florida White: This East-coast hybrid was derived from the Polish, Dutch and New Zealand White principally for use by scientists. This smallish rabbit is always solid white and considerably hardy. The Florida White is a compact, rather short, close-coupled rabbit with a pleasant appearance and disposition.

Californian: The West-coast counterpart to the Florida White, perhaps, is the Californian, a pure white rabbit with black Himalayan markings on the body. This is a Roaring Twenties rabbit creation, achieved by crossing a Himalayan and a Chinchilla. The body is medium long appearing full and somewhat rounded. Like any good West-coast beach bunny, this rabbit is well proportioned and invitingly shaped.

Beveren: Beveren is a small town in Belgium where the so-named was first bred in the early 1900s. Its initial popularity in England was with butchers, as opposed to pet shop keepers, as meat was very scarce during the First World War. While no more musical than other rabbits, the Beveren's frame is mandolin-shaped and enjoys being stroked (or strummed). Considered one of the largest of the fur breeds, the Beveren can weigh up to ten pounds.

Rex: Differing from the normal-furred rabbits, the Rex varieties exhibit a soft velvety coat achieved by guard hairs of equal length to the undercoat fur. The whiskers on all varieties are curly and shortish. Originally considered runts in normal-furred litters, the Rex eventually secured mutant status and began to be exhibited as a true-breeding oddity, not merely a half-furred outcast. Among the many Rex colors are opal, lynx, sable, seal, blue, castor, chinchilla, and others. Colors often suffer from the lack of density of the coat. Breeding problems are often encountered in the Rex varieties.

Sable: This small-sized rabbit is a well-furred, good-eared little darling who sports a very rich sepia-brown color, which extends as deep as possible. The eyes are brown with a distinct ruby glow.

Jersey Wooly: This Angora-type rabbit is a newcomer to the exhibition world. The wool, which covers the entire body, is one to three inches in length and as dense as possible; when considering the relative density of a specimen's coat, blow into the wool. Overall it is a compact, short-coupled rabbit with a well-rounded head. The ears are well furred with tufts at the ends, though not so exaggerated to be considered tassels. Various colors of wool and eyes are possible.

WHERE TO BUY

Depending on the breed and color of your preferred rabbit, your resources to locate a fine specimen may be limited. Never compromise and take home a sickly animal or a representative of a breed that you don't really admire. Remember that happiness with a pet is a mutual thing—you're responsible for providing for the animal for the duration of its life. Adult animals are the less likely to be adopted should you decide that you're not compatible or are discontent with your furry charge.

For all but the rare or uncommon breed, your local pet shop is your best source. Apply strict criteria to any establishment that is selling live animals. Demand overall cleanliness in the surrounds; look for alert and healthy rabbits; insist upon intelligent answers to all your questions (from the proprietor, more so than the rabbits). It is fine, incidentally, to interrogate the rabbits at length, just don't insist upon intelligent responses; a promising jitter of the foreface seems appropriate. A shabbily run, untidy operation is

indicative of the health and hardiness of the stock. Always know as much as possible before purchasing a pet, be aware of what a healthy specimen looks like, how large a six-week-old bunny can be, what characteristics are important in your chosen breed, etc. If you are looking for a particular breed or a less-popular color variety of a known breed, a breeder may be your only promising outlet. Breeders generally are dedicated fanciers and prove to

Never pick up a rabbit by its ears. Instead, grasp the loose skin over the shoulders with one hand and lift the hindquarters with the other hand.

English Angora rabbit. This breed of rabbit is distinguished by the abundant tassels and fringes on its ears. In the rabbit fancy, the fur of Angora-type rabbits is known as wool. Photo by Vincent Serbin.

Oh, those ears! This assortment of Lop rabbits portrays the unique appeal of the long-eared lagomorph. Pictured: French Lop, English Lop, Mini Lop, and Holland Lop. Photo by Bruce Crook.

be highly knowledgable; likewise, they are equally interested in you and the kind of environment and home you intend to give your new pet.

ALL RABBITS ARE LOVABLE

After you familiarize yourself with all the rabbit breeds that are available to hobbyists, you will no doubt give consideration to the question, "Which one is best for *me*?" All rabbits are equally lovable and all have their own particular appeal. Most likely your decision will be influenced by the rabbit that has "that special something." Your most important consideration, however, should be the selection of a rabbit that is healthy and sound.

BEST AGE TO BUY

The best age to buy a rabbit is when he is from eight to ten weeks old.

Carefully observe the rabbit you intend to buy. Notice his eyes: they should be bright and clear. His nose should not be runny. If a rabbit has sniffles or sneezes, better pass him up. The coat should be sleek and evenly distributed. If there are stains or discolorations around the vent, they would indicate diarrhea—a sure reason for rejection.

Whether to buy a male or female depends on the buyer. If you buy a female you may wish to breed her later, and the experience of helping to raise a batch of bunnies is a memorable one. Keep in mind, however, that properly caring for your rabbit family will require a good bit of your time and energy.

HANDLING

When you first get your new bunny, you will probably want to hold him. This is very natural since he is one of the most cuddly of all pets. Happily, handling a rabbit makes him even more tame and friendly. Make sure that you are doing it correctly. If your rabbit is still a baby, he should be picked up with both hands. Slip one hand under his chest, and use the other to support his hindquarters. When your rabbit has grown older, you should use one hand to hold the loose skin over his shoulders and pick him up with the other hand under his rump. *Never* pick up a rabbit by the ears.

Your new rabbit is like a new baby and should be treated as such. It is best not to handle him too much when you first get him home. Don't invite the whole neighborhood in to pet him either. You will be tempted to do this because you'll want to show your new pet off, but this should be done gradually as he becomes more accustomed to having people around him.

Before small children handle the bunny, you must explain that he is different from the stuffed bunny they may toss around in their room, or pick up by the ears or tail. Show them the proper way to handle him.

If these few tips are observed, the rabbit's transition from the pet shop to your home will be a happy and a healthy one.

Care

Once your new bunny has settled down in his new home you will want to try hard to make him happy. But when it comes to food, you must temper your affections. Your bunny must be kept on a proper diet and you must try hard to follow it. Although bunnies are usually associated with goodies like candy and chocolate-covered eggs, you certainly should not feed your pet such sweets.

FEEDING GUIDELINES

Do not overfeed your pet. Twice a day, morning and evening, is enough. Pelletized rabbit food, available at your pet shop, should form the mainstay of your pet's diet. This food provides a convenient balanced diet and is used successfully by countless numbers of rabbit keepers. You can supplement the prepared food with an occasional nibble of stale bread. Greens should be offered to your pet on a limited basis only, and be sure that any fresh food items are thoroughly washed before they are served to your pet. Some hobbyists like to provide their rabbits with a salt lick or spool, while others feel that prepared rabbit food contains a sufficient amount of this element.

Avoid giving him leftovers or in-between-meal snacks. And you should not, of course, give him meat.

Your rabbit is a decided vegetarian!

Keep plenty of fresh water available at all times. It is best to serve your rabbit's water in a water bottle that attaches to the side of the cage. In this way the water cannot become soiled by droppings or bedding material. Feeding dishes should be deep and heavy so that your pet cannot tip them.

ACCLIMATION

There is more to feeding and taking care of a rabbit than meets the eye. Don't just set the food in front of him and walk away; try to keep him company. Speak to him in a gentle voice, show him that you are friendly.

When you want him to come to you, call him softly by name—don't shout. When he comes to you, reward him; eventually he will grow more friendly. As you stroke him, move your hand in the same direction as the lie of the fur—don't ruffle it.

Rabbits generally get along fine with other pets. However, exercise caution when introducing your bunny. Do not give your other pets any opportunity to harm the bunny. Some rabbit-keepers claim it's quite a sight to see a rabbit playing with a large dog, even leaping over his big friend in his exuberance! Such behavior, however, is more the exception than the rule.

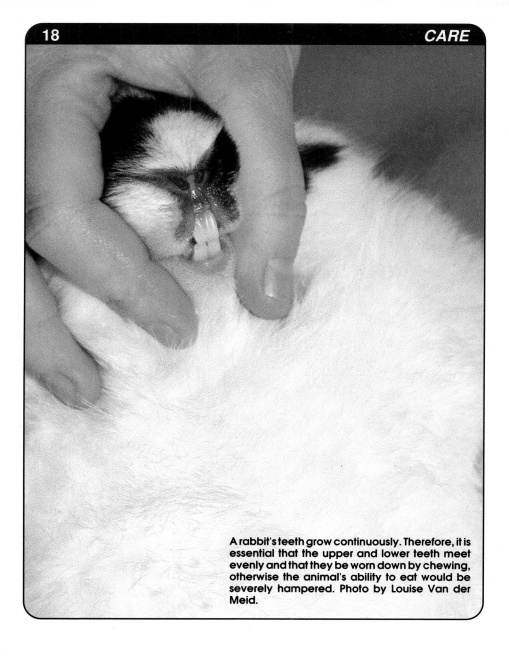

A rabbit's teeth grow continuously. Therefore, it is essential that the upper and lower teeth meet evenly and that they be worn down by chewing, otherwise the animal's ability to eat would be severely hampered. Photo by Louise Van der Meid.

Top: There is a variety of rabbit treats from which you can choose. Photo courtesy Vitakraft. Bottom: Pelleted feed is part of a rabbit's basic diet. Photo courtesy of Hagen.

HOUSING

Your rabbit will live in a house within a home: you will keep him in your own home, but he will have a house of his own—a hutch. This will give him all the comforts of expansive living, and save you the trouble of finding him when he has crawled into some hidden corner.

The hutch can be in or out of doors. It depends upon you. If outdoors, of course, it will require more weatherproofing. The pen should be large enough to allow the rabbit to exercise. It should be at least four and one-half feet wide, two and one-half feet high, and two feet deep. It should be divided into two parts: two-thirds of it a screened-in "front yard," one-third, a closed-in "bedroom." A rabbit demands privacy for his sleeping and breeding. Therefore, the bedroom should be closed in. A flap of burlap will provide a simple door and protect him from drafts.

If you decide to keep the hutch outdoors, place it in a spot that gets some sun, but remember to avoid direct sun because it will make the pen too hot. Your rabbit doesn't require much heat, but he does need a lot of sunlight.

The hutch should be built at least two feet off the ground, with a sloping roof and a slight overhang; rain will then run off the back. For added protection, canvas flaps can be attached to all four sides and lowered when the weather is bad. The roof should be hinged to permit easy cleaning.

The "front yard" should be enclosed in one-half inch wire mesh screen; this not only makes the cage mouse-proof, it prevents stray cats from poking their claws through.

For bedding, use a material that is soft. Hay is one choice; straw and wood shavings can also be used.

HOUSEKEEPING

Regardless of the material used for your rabbit's bedding, it should always be clean. Replace the bedding two or three times weekly, except during breeding or after the birth of baby rabbits.

Rabbits are among some of the cleanest animals in the world, and they always assist their owners in keeping their home clean and neat. Your pet will usually dirty only one corner of his hutch. Try to clean this corner every day.

The entire living area should be cleaned thoroughly at least once a week. Scrub it with a solution of mild disinfectant.

Cleanliness is the best insurance for the health of your rabbit. You are lucky to have a pet that is so clean by nature, one that is easy to take care of. Help him along with these few simple guidelines and you will be helping him to a happy and healthy life.

EXERCISE

Rabbits traditionally cut a pretty trim figure, but this is because in the wild they get plenty of exercise. Domestic rabbits should get as much exercise as possible to keep them from getting fat or pot-bellied.

If the hutch is big enough, he can get much of his exercise just running and hopping about. It is better, however, to take him out of his quarters just as much as possible. A fenced-in garden or yard can make a fine rabbit playground; just remember that your pet should be under supervision at all times during the play period.

Never let him out in cold or wet weather, as he might get a chill. If you do not have a fenced-in garden or yard, you can take him out for a walk. Provide him with a properly sized figure-eight cat harness and a light lead, and let him accompany you on your walks. (It should be noted that some rabbits enjoy such expeditions, while others detest it.)

Another way to provide exercise for your bunny is to give him the run of the house. Be sure to provide a plastic pan of cat litter and situate it in a central location. Put some of your pet's droppings in the litter pan to attract his attention, and take him to the pan regularly. Hopefully, he will catch on.

SAFETY TIPS

Naturally, you will want to take every step to ensure your rabbit's safety and well-being—both in the indoor environment and in the outdoors as well.

Periodically check your pet's housing for any signs of wear-and-tear. A protruding piece of cage wire can cause a painful scratch if your pet brushes against it. By the same token, worn-out materials can become a virtual haven for parasites and other pests.

Food utensils, particularly the feeding dishes, should be heavy in weight to prevent tipping; a lightweight glass or ceramic dish can be shoved about and shattered by a rabbit's vigorous hopping movements.

When you let your pet out of its cage for playtime and/or an exercise session, make sure that you are ready nearby to keep an eye on him. Remember that rabbits love to gnaw, and they are not always discriminating in the object of this favorite pastime: chewing on an electrical cord indoors or a toxic object outdoors can lead to quick and unnecessary death.

POISONOUS PLANTS

Contrary to a commonly held assumption, rabbits do not always reject poisonous plants. If your pet is permitted outdoors, you should familiarize yourself with the wild plants that grow in your neighborhood. Plants to be avoided include foxglove, yew, creeping buttercup, and all plants from bulbs. Generally, do not let your pet eat unknown plant matter. Rabbit keepers should also be aware that milkweed, a plant found in eastern North America is toxic to all rabbits. Symptoms of milkweed poisoning are evidenced by paralysis. Treatment and cure for milkweed poisoning involve a slow process. Veterinary care is an absolute must.

Red-eyed white Holland Lop. Averaging three pounds in weight, this rabbit is the smallest of all the Lop rabbit breeds. Photo by Burkhard Kahl.

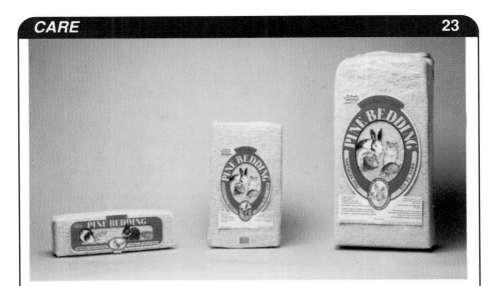

Top: Bedding material can be purchased at your pet shop. Photo courtesy of Hagen. Bottom: A pair of American Fuzzy Lops. Photo by Isabelle Francais.

Health

If you give your rabbit the proper care and attention, hopefully he will maintain a sound state of health. Most diseases result from the lack of proper care, unsanitary living conditions, bad ventilation, or too much, too little, or improper food. If your rabbit does not respond to the treatments suggested here, call the veterinarian.

COMMON COLD

Correctly known as contagious rhinitis. Symptoms are a runny nose and sneezing. The nasal discharge can become thick and yellow as the disease progresses. Kept warm and dry, rabbits frequently recover by themselves. In severe cases, the use of sulfa or penicillin, or one of the mycins, is usually effective.

CONSTIPATION

A warm mash of boiled potatoes with the skins left on, or clover leaves mixed with bran, can help to alleviate this condition. A modest increase in the amount of greens that you feed to your pet may also help. (It goes without saying that clean fresh water should be available.)

DIARRHEA

Immediately eliminate the greens in the diet and increase dry food. Sometimes a little drained boiled rice does wonders for the sufferer.

CANKER

This ear ailment is sometimes not noticeable externally. If your pet begins to shake his head constantly or scratch at his ears, or if you notice any signs of inflammation, he should be examined for canker. For treatment, begin by wiping out the ears with hydrogen peroxide applied with a cotton-tipped swab. Afterwards, dust the ear with an appropriate antibiotic. Avoid using preparations that are formulated for dogs. If you are uncertain about selecting the right medicament, consult your veterinarian.

Like all animals with fur coats, rabbits get fleas. The best way to get rid of them is to use an insecticidal preparation, available from a veterinarian or pet shop. Make sure that none gets into the rabbit's eyes. Additionally, clean and treat the hutch thoroughly, and change the bedding.

POT BELLY

Pot belly is a familiar condition, especially in urban rabbits, and one of the best protections against it is to make sure that the rabbit gets plenty of exercise. It is caused by inactivity and by eating green foods when they are damp or moldy. If the rabbit is afflicted with pot belly, give him *very little* green food; also decrease the amount of his pelletized food. Give him more than ample opportunity for exercise.

EYE INFECTIONS

Domestic rabbits are rather susceptible to eye problems, primarily infections caused by dust and/or other flying matter that accumulates in the tear ducts. As a result of the blockage caused by the dirt gathered, fluid fills the eye pocket and subsequently flows down the rabbit's cheeks. What owner can dare see his bunny weeping? Prevention of dust accumulation should be stressed, as a cure is never as easy as prevention. Often only one eye is affected, although some unfortunate rabbits suffer an infection in both eyes. Eye baths, prescribed by a veterinarian, are frequently required to treat the infection. The skin and fur around the eyes, likewise, may be affected. Drafts may also be responsible for eye infections.

PNEUMONIA

A rabbit well cared for and properly fed rarely encounters this serious illness. Keep the rabbit's environment consistent, including the ambient temperature; sudden changes in temperature diminish a rabbit's natural resistance. A listless, unhappy, unhungry bunny requires your attention, as these are signs of pneumonia, in addition to mucus around the mouth and nasal passages. The assistance of a veterinarian is essential, as most rabbits die within a few days of contracting the illness.

SORE HOCKS

While sore hocks may be a simple matter, for your rabbit it is no laughing matter. Skin, tender and cracked (possibly scabbing), covers the infected hind limb where the fur has been rubbed away. Since the smaller rabbits have larger foot padding on the hind feet, the larger breeds are more typically affected. Cleaning and applying an antiseptic ointment help the rabbit to recovery. Veterinary advice is also recommended.

SLOBBERS, SCABBY FACE, AND HUTCH BURN

More reminiscent of Dick Tracy characters than rabbit conditions, these three problems require serious commentary. Slobbers is caused by abscesses of the mouth; the drooling lagomorph has worse worries than just bad table manners, slobbering rather continually. Little can be done for slobbers, and the affected animal will need to be put down. Hutch burn, commonly known as vent disease, is caused by dirt contacting the sex organ of the rabbit. The infected organ then becomes scabby and later purulent. Not surprisingly, infected rabbits exhibit a certain reluctance to mate (which is fortunate for the spared mate, who could become contaminated). Coprophagy may accompany hutch burn, and scabby face results from the rabbit taking pellets from the anus. A veterinarian should be contacted as soon as possible.

Contrary to popular belief, carrots are *not* the main staple of a rabbit's diet. Greenfoods can cause digestive disturbance and should be offered on a limited basis only. Photo by Louise Van der Meid.

No matter what type of bunny you decide upon, you can be certain that it will provide you with pleasure and satisfaction. Photo by Burkhard Kahl.

Breeding

If you are at all familiar with rabbits, then you are aware of their great capacity to reproduce. There have been litters as large as eighteen rabbits, but relax—the average litter is about six.

If you wish to raise a family of rabbits, keep in mind that doing so requires an investment of time and money on your part, and most importantly, consideration of what you will do with all of the youngsters.

If you have two rabbits, the

Sexing a female rabbit: the sex organ is slit-like in appearance and located close to the rear.

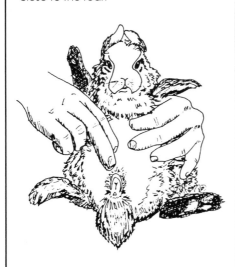

prospect of your having a little family are good, provided that you have a male and a female. How do you tell if your rabbits are boy or girl rabbits? In rabbits that are less than eight to ten weeks of age, it is difficult to tell sometimes. The process of determining the sex of an animal is called sexing. In some animals, like birds and snakes, sexing is almost impossible to tell from simple observation. Fortunately with rabbits, sexing is pretty easy. Just look at the bunny's private parts to tell whether it is male or female. Gently pull forward the skin directly in front of your furry friend's genitals and back from the tail end. If you have a male rabbit, his little penis will be visible, and maybe the testicles too; if you have a female rabbit, her slit-like organ, which is closer to the rear than the male's penis, will open up when pressure is exerted. Only a more experienced person can tell the sex of a very young rabbit. Generally, though, the male has a broader head and is somewhat smaller than the female; unfortunately head shape is variable even within a litter, so this rule is not very reliable, even in adults.

A female rabbit, or doe, as she is called, can be bred as early as six months old, although eight months is preferable. Also, a doe should not be allowed more than three litters a year. If she is a healthy rabbit, she will be able to have babies until she is three or four years old. The gestation period of the rabbit is quite short: about 30 to 32 days.

When you are ready to breed your rabbit, introduce the doe to the male, or buck as he is called, in the buck's cage. If they seem friendly, leave them undisturbed. Sometimes, a breeding is not successful on the first attempt; in this case, several visits from the doe may be necessary.

If you have any doubts about whether or not the mating has taken place, stop bringing the doe to the buck. Let a few days go by. Then bring the doe back to the buck's hutch. If she seems irritated or growls at him, it is quite likely that mating has already taken place. After mating, the doe becomes rather upset at further attention from the male.

The mother-to-be needs adequate rest and proper food during her pregnancy. Make life comfortable during this month. You may wish to offer a vitamin supplement.

About a week before the babies are due to be born, provide the doe with a nest box and nesting material. She will arrange the nest herself, and will add to its warmth and comfort by padding it with bits of her own fur. During this time, do not disturb the doe or the cage, except for essentials such as feeding. Don't be concerned if she becomes increasingly nervous as the big day approaches.

THE NEW FAMILY

It is important that you do not disturb the doe or her babies. Try to restrain your curiosity, at least for the first five days. If you *must* take a peek, choose a time when the mother is out of the nest and make it a quick look. Make sure no light shines on the babies because, at this time, their eyes are highly sensitive.

The doe knows by instinct how to raise her young, and if she is interfered with and someone tries to handle her babies, she may disown or even kill them. This may sound like strange behavior from a mother who loves her children, but it is not uncommon in the rabbit world. Your rabbit, no matter how fond she may be of you, is instinctively distrustful during this sensitive period.

Baby rabbits are born with their eyes closed and are hairless. In a few days, though, these little infants will have grown a soft protective fuzz, and in a couple of weeks they will have developed a coat. By this time their eyes will be open and their ears perked up.

After three weeks, the new bunnies will be hopping about on their own. As soon as they can do this, they will begin to feed themselves. During this period they should not be weaned; this comes later: at about six to eight weeks. Then, the youngsters may nibble on pelletized rabbit food. Some hobbyists like to offer the young rabbits a vitamin supplement. Never offer any kinds of greens to immature rabbits.

A black Silver Fox doe. All domestic rabbits are descended from the common wild European rabbit. Photo by Michael Gilroy.

A Dutch rabbit and his loving owner. Cute and cuddlesome, the rabbit is the pet of choice for many youngsters. Photo by Vincent Serbin.

Conclusion

To own a rabbit is to love a rabbit. Playful, mischievous, and most entertaining, rabbits return the affection of children and grownups in a manner all their own. They are like no other pet. These furry little bundles are quiet—so quiet—yet active! They're never still for a moment. Noses quiver, legs thump, ears twitch. It's all symptomatic of the happy, well-housed and well-cared-for rabbit.

Children love their long-eared friends on sight. They learn to care for them as they play with them. Responsibility is acquired in a simple, straightforward manner, and your children will be better for it.

Many is the family that bought a rabbit or acquired one as a gift and then looked for a second. Bunnies are delightful to hold and handle and watch and enjoy. Rare, indeed, is the house that once had rabbits but has them no more. Rabbits are so easy to care for, made of such sturdy stuff, so enjoyable to have around, that they have come to rival dogs and cats in popularity. They are relatively inexpensive to maintain. They take up little space. They're clean. And they're forever happy.

You have only to look in the bright eyes of a rabbit to love him. Stroke his fur and feel the beat of his heart and you won't want to put him down.

He seems to have been created to be fondled and loved. His lengthy ears search for your kind word, and his ever-twitching nose converses with you in rabbit language. He's been bred to be a pet, to receive and to return affection. This he does most nobly.

As a proud and fond rabbit owner, you can extend your interest to the fascinating world of exhibition and other rabbit activities. Whether you live in North America, Great Britain, or other parts of the world, there are national organizations that serve the rabbit community. Breed specialist clubs and membership organizations sponsor a variety of intriguing, ear-raising events that typically are open to all rabbit fanciers, though perhaps not to their particular rabbit variety. For more information, fanciers are encouraged to contact either the American Rabbit Breeders' Association (ARBA) or the British Rabbit Council (BRC). Both of these successful organizations have been providing excellent service for over half a century. Classes vary at shows from scrub rabbits (non-pedigreed) to full pedigreed rabbits, so everyone is welcome to get involved. Think of the fun possible when you get together with other enthusiastic rabbit fanciers and exchange bunny truths and tails! And the rabbits like it too!

Bibliography

ALL ABOUT RABBITS
By Howard Hirschhorn
TFH M-543
Contents: What About Rabbits?
Rabbit Housing. Shipment Of Rabbits.
Feeding. Health. Breeding. Rabbit
Handling. Rabbit Clubs. Standards And
Shows. Profitable Commercial Aspects
Of Raising Animals. Final Thoughts On
Rabbit Theory.
Audience: An excellent book for
someone who buys his first rabbit and
who is interested in breeding or
showing the rabbit. Written on an 8-
12th grade level.
Hard cover, 5½ x 8", 96 pages
32 color photos; 39 black and white
photos.

STARTING RIGHT WITH RABBITS
By Mervin F. Roberts
TFH PS-796
Contents: Introduction. Rabbit
Cousins. Rabbits in Legend and
Literature. What Rabbits Eat. Choosing
a Pet Rabbit. Handling Rabbits.
Diseases. Breeding. Genetics.
Economics. Odd Facts about Rabbits.
Audience: This fine new book leads
beginners by the hand and guides
them in the right way to get started in
rabbit-keeping. The excellent
photography includes both pertinent
how-to photos and beautiful portraits of
different rabbit varieties. Age 13 and
up.
Hard cover   112 pages
Completely illustrated throughout;
includes over 75 full-color photos.

DWARF RABBITS
By Gunter Flauhaus
TFH H-1073
Contents: The History of Rabbits.
Origin of the Dwarf Rabbit. Breeds of
Rabbits. Designation of the Sexes.
Purchasing of Dwarf Rabbits. Housing.
Care. Feeding. Multiplying and
Breeding. Diseases.
Audience: This book is the
introductory text for owners (and
potential owners) of rabbits that have
been bred down to smaller size than
most of the breeds commonly available
as pets; fine value for beginners.
Hard cover, 5½ x 8", 128 pages
Illustrated with full-color and black and
white photos.

ENCYCLOPEDIA OF PET RABBITS
By D. Robinson
TFH H-984
Contents: This is the most thorough,
comprehensive, and descriptive text
available on rabbits. Every aspect of
successful rabbit husbandry is covered
in detail. In addition, almost all of the
recognized breeds, and many of the
color varieties within each breed, are
represented in large full-color
photographs.
Audience: This excellent book is
designed to help all rabbit enthusiasts,
beginners and experienced owners
alike.
Hard cover; 5½ x 8"; 320 pages
231 full-color photos, 52 black and
white photos.